CONTENTS

Spring

It is Spring on the farm.
At dawn the cock crows.

He wakes everyone up.

by Sally Hewitt
Photographs by Chris Fairclough

W
FRANKLIN WATTS
LONDON•SYDNEY

First published in 2004 by Franklin Watts
96 Leonard Street, London EC2A 4XD

Franklin Watts Australia
45-51 Huntley Street, Alexandria, NSW 2015

© Franklin Watts 2004

Editor: Kate Newport
Art director: Jonathan Hair
Photographer: Chris Fairclough
Designer: Steve Prosser

A CIP catalogue record for this book
is available from the British Library

ISBN 0 7496 4821 X

Printed in Malaysia

The farmer gets up early all
year round.

Baby lambs are
born in the Spring.

Most drink milk
from their mother.

Some are fed with a bottle.

Cows and their calves munch the fresh green grass.

New shoots of wheat push up
through the ploughed earth.

Summer

In Summer, everyone goes to the agricultural show.

The farmers show off
their animals and crops.

You can see the prize-
winning bull.

Fields of wheat turn gold
in the Summer sun.

The combine harvester is
used to cut the wheat.

In Summer, the sheep are hot in their woolly coats.

It is the time for shearing.

The sheepdog pants
to keep cool.

Autumn

By Autumn, the harvest
is over.

The fields are ploughed
and ready for a new crop.

In the orchard, everyone helps to pick the apples.

They are ripe and juicy!

Potatoes are dug up from
under the earth.

Autumn rain makes the farmyard very muddy.

The baby lambs have grown.

They eat grass with
their mothers.

Winter

In Winter, new crops are
sown in the ploughed fields.

Birds swoop down looking
for seeds to eat.

There is time to mend broken fences.

Snow covers the apple
trees in the orchard.

The ground is frozen hard.

The sheep need to be given extra food.

A hot drink helps the farmer warm up after a morning on the farm.

INDEX